TALKING TAILS

The Incredible Connection Between People and Their Pets

ANN LOVE & JANE DRAKE
ILLUSTRATED BY BILL SLAVIN

TUNDRA BOOKS

For Alex, Angus, Nellie, and Skookum
– A.L. & J.D.
For Karen and all her cougars
– B.S.

Acknowledgments

With thanks to . . .

Birds – Budweiser, Casper, Chippy-Bobby, Molson, Ruckus; **Cats** – Bojangles, Holly, Jasper, Kiki, Kitza, Louie, Luther, Mabel, Mabel Two, Milo, Miss You, Naoko, Oliver, Quincy, Roger, Runtlin,' Tom, Treacle, Woozie; **Dogs** – Abbey, Archer, Aztec, Beazley, Blues, Bosch, Darius, the Dude, Guinness, Humbert, Jackie, Jessie, Lolita, Neptune, Poochie, Portia, Riley, Silas, Silverdog, Stella, Tagish, Tasha, Willie, Wolfie; **Fish** – Baby Blue, Boots, Bop Bop, Choo Choo, Dora, Firecracker, Fluffy, Frixie, Golden Peaches, Honey Sunset, Kisses, Maurice, Perseus, Pineapple; **Guinea Pigs** – Carter, Cleats, Josephine, Napoleon, Rosie; **Hamsters** – Buchanan, Ginger, Nibbles, Speed; **Rabbits** – Hoppy, Mulberry; **Rats** – Peanut, Whiskers . . . and to all who loved them.

Many thanks to Kathy Lowinger and Sue Tate, who share our affection for four-legged friends. A *woof* of thanks to the Tundra team. It's great fun being part of your pack!

Authors' Note

In the time line, we use modern place names, such as Iran and Italy, followed by the historical names for peoples, such as the Persians and the Romans. Where we couldn't pinpoint an exact date, we selected one mid-timeframe and used the symbol *c* for *circa* to indicate that our date is approximate.

Text copyright © 2010 by Ann Love and Jane Drake
Illustrations copyright © 2010 by Bill Slavin

Published in Canada by Tundra Books,
75 Sherbourne Street, Toronto, Ontario M5A 2P9
Published in the United States by Tundra Books of Northern New York,
P.O. Box 1030, Plattsburgh, New York 12901

Library of Congress Control Number: 2009928991

Library and Archives Canada Cataloguing in Publication

Love, Ann

Talking tails : the incredible connection between people and their pets / Ann
Love, Jane Drake ; illustrated by Bill Slavin.

Includes index.

ISBN 978–0–88776–884–2

1. Pets – Juvenile literature. 2. Human-animal relationships – Juvenile literature. I. Drake, Jane II. Slavin, Bill III. Title.

SF416.2.L68 2010   j636.088'7   C2009–902977–4

We acknowledge the financial support of the Government of Canada through the Book Publishing Industry Development Program (BPIDP) and that of the Government of Ontario through the Ontario Media Development Corporation's Ontario Book Initiative.
We further acknowledge the support of the Canada Council for the Arts and the Ontario Arts Council for our publishing program.

ONTARIO ARTS COUNCIL
CONSEIL DES ARTS DE L'ONTARIO

Medium: Pen and ink with watercolor on paper

Design: Leah Springate

Printed and bound in China

1 2 3 4 5 6   15 14 13 12 11 10

C O N T E N T S

PETS AND PEOPLE: HEARTS AND SMARTS

The Heart of the Matter

Let's tour this store and zoom in on the interactions between pets and people, then ask ourselves: *Should we join the billions who share their lives with pets?*

In aisle one, an attendant hands Natalie a young guinea pig. Cupping her hands around the soft wiggling body, she smiles at her dad. She's chosen her birthday gift already.

In the reference section, Sophia pours over horse-training books while her mom looks for one on housebreaking dogs. Angus, their puppy, strains on his leash, confused and excited by all the wonderful smells. Everyone passing pats his silky head and says, *"Ahhhhhhh!"*

Lukas watches a clown fish dart among the sea anemones in a saltwater tank. He's fascinated by their symbiotic relationship,

c. 100,000 B.C.

EURASIA: a bone to pick? Scientists think that dogs and gray wolves separate into distinct species

so is not impressed when his parents point to a nearby tank of goldfish.

Hailey walks past cages of lovebirds, cockatoos, budgies, and canaries, stopping in front of a big parrot. "Polly wanna cracker?" she whispers. The parrot yells back, "Polly wanna carrot!" Hailey grabs a box of songbird seed and heads for the checkout, giggling.

In the grooming department, Paco's two standard poodles wait patiently, leashes slack. Elegant and confident, they know they'll look spectacular when they're washed and clipped. They ignore the antics of a young terrier covered in shampoo.

A crowd gathers around a pen of rare, purebred, lavender Persian cats. They tumble over one another, meowing and squeaking. A senior couple looking for a mature cat goes straight to the adoption center.

Jack stares at a snoozing collie puppy and is swept back thirteen years to when Riley joined the family. At first, the dog was forbidden to climb on the furniture, but Riley discovered that he could sneak onto the basement couch and

leap off before anyone saw him. As he got older, he was caught sometimes. Now that Riley is frail, Jack lifts him onto the couch and lets him rest.

Come and explore the unique connection between people and their pets.

c. 14,000 B.C.	*c.* 12,000 B.C.	*c.* 10,500 B.C.	*c.* 7500 B.C.
● GERMANY: dogs are buried with their masters at Bonn-Oberkassel	● FRANCE: an artist carves a horse's head out of mammoth ivory	● MIDDLE EAST: humans domesticate their first wild animals, starting with goats and sheep	● CYPRUS: pet cats are buried beside people at Shillourokambos

Pets on the Brain

What is an "amygdala" (pronounced *ah-MIG-dah-lah*)? Could it be ancient Egyptian for the collar worn by a sacred cat? Or a soothing word whispered by snake charmers while taming cobras?

Actually, amygdala is the name for a structure inside your brain, the shape and size of an almond, important to your memory, your sense of smell, and the way you express your feelings. When you nuzzle your pet and get that warm, soft, caring feeling, the connections between your amygdala and the rest of your brain are sizzling.

Does your pet feel the same warm fuzzies for you? A seventeenth-century French philosopher, René Descartes, believed that dogs were like machines with no feelings. For years, scientists argued that only humans had emotions, but modern scientists disagree. Dogs, cats, and all mammals have amygdalas as well as thinking upper brains, or cerebral cortexes. Although less developed and interconnected than human brains, advanced mammal brains have the capacity for anger, fear,

c. 7000 B.C.

EUROPE: hunters train dogs to stalk prey along coastlines

c. 6400 B.C.

CHINA: mourners bury human and dog remains along with two flutes

happiness, and maybe even true love. However, most mammals keep their tender feelings for their own kind: giraffes, polar bears, and bats likely won't come when you call. But dogs and cats feel socially comfortable in human families – also because of signals from their brains – and extend affection back to us.

Fish, reptiles, and birds have more primitive brains, with tiny or no amygdalas or cerebral cortexes. Even so, scientists know these animals can use their little brains to perform advanced activities, such as territorial singing in birds. But it's unlikely they're able to return our kind of love. That may be why some kids find they bond differently to their pet dog or cat than to their goldfish or budgie. Even if they never get back an "I love you," most kids adore their chosen pet – fish, snake, bird, cat, or dog.

You know your own heart – and it's in your head!

c. 4000 B.C.

c. 3000 B.C.

UKRAINE: riders control their horses with bridles that anthropologists think were made with pieces of rope and antler
TURKEY: ancestors of the Anatolian shepherd dog guard flocks of sheep and their sleeping herdsmen

EGYPT: farmers encourage cats to hunt birds, to fish, and to rid grain storehouses of rodents

7

DIFFERENT PETS FOR DIFFERENT FOLKS

Exotics: Rare and Unusual Pets

What do a bear on a Europe-bound World War I troop ship, a giraffe in an ancient Roman villa, and a monkey wintering in the Arctic in 1845 have in common? These animals are examples of exotic pets plucked from their home environments. Some were kept for amusement or companionship; others earned their keep in circuses or by street entertainment. All died far from their natural habitats.

Today, celebrities sometimes use exotic pets as fashion accessories. One bought a Bengal tiger — but, oh, my gosh — when it grew too big, she sent it off to her property in Nevada. Then she wanted a kinkajou — a cute rainforest mammal imported from South America. It turned out that Baby Luv, the kink, not only bit, but was an illegal pet in California.

c. 2000 B.C.

c. 1800 B.C.

EGYPT: pet birds, including parrots, are kept in cages

EGYPT: grave painters portray dogs that look like modern breeds

8

Owning a rare or exotic pet can be complicated: most will never become domesticated like cats or dogs. Beyond their specialized food, habitat, and veterinary needs, some grow too big or unruly. Zoos or farms often can't absorb discarded pets, and releasing them into the "wild" isn't fair. Forced to fend for themselves, exotic pets can starve or upset the local balance of nature. Some, such as red-eared slider turtles, become serious pests known as invasive species. If you're keen on owning an unusual pet, make sure you get it from a reputable supplier who follows the rules.

WINNIE THE POOH: EXOTIC PET?

When a World War I troop train stopped in White River, Ontario, and Lieutenant Harry Colebourn bought an orphaned bear cub, no one knew he'd inspire the classic stories of Winnie the Pooh. Colebourn named the bear Winnipeg, after his hometown, and left "Winnie" in a London zoo when his brigade shipped out to France. Writer A.A. Milne and his son, Christopher Robin, visited Winnie many times. Christopher was even allowed inside the bear's cage. Winnie became Pooh in Milne's *When We Were Very Young*. And Milne based the characters of Piglet, Tigger, Roo, Kanga, and Eeyore on Christopher's stuffed animals.

c. 1700 B.C.

c. 1120 B.C.   *c.* 1100 B.C.

CRETE: Minoan people enjoy rodeos featuring bull riding

CHINA: a manuscript records that four-foot-tall Tibetan dogs, ancestors of mastiffs, are sent as a gift to Emperor Zhou Wu Wang

GREECE: Homer praises Iberian horses in his song-poem *The Iliad*

Pets of a Feather

"**T**ell me again about Casper." Maddy loves the stories Dad tells us about the budgie he had when he was a boy. She marvels at Casper's vocabulary ("Jimmy, shut the door!" "Boys, stop that!" "Pretty Casper!"). She can picture Grandma's kitchen, the bird, Dad, and his brothers. The best story is about Casper landing in Uncle Steve's cereal, Puffed Rice flying all over the table. Casper used to ride on Dad's shoulder and fly back to his cage from anywhere in the house. *What a bird!*

Maddy and Dad finally talk Mom into getting a budgie, and the preparations begin. First, they buy a cage with a stand so the bird can live in the kitchen, where the action is. Grandma sews a skirt for around the bottom of the cage — it will catch some of the seeds and debris the budgie will toss out. Casper II must have a water dispenser, seed tray, and millet to clip on the cage. And he needs several small bowls for fresh bits of tropical fruit or berries; sprouted greens or herbs and raw vegetables

c. 1000 B.C.

EGYPT: mummified cats confirm the high status of domestic felines
MIDDLE EAST: Phoenician sea traders bring peacocks from India to Egypt

such as carrots, peas, or zucchini; plus one bowl for bathing. Maddy sprinkles fine gravel for birds on the floor of the cage and clips on a piece of calcium-rich cuttlefish bone. Dad remembers that his Casper loved to chatter and peck at a little mirror – something that kept him company when the family was out.

At the pet store, Maddy watches the antics in a cage full of brilliantly colored young budgerigars. Mom likes the olive yellow one, but Maddy knows a true Casper must be cobalt blue. Adult males have blue ceres (where the nostrils open at the base of the beak), but the young ones don't. Maddy eliminates one cobalt blue budgie with white around the cere – it's probably a female. Eventually the salesperson gently places Maddy's choice in a carrying box, and Dad adds a book on budgies to their purchase.

When they arrive home, Maddy starts training Casper immediately. She chirps in her best budgie voice: "Dad – Jimmy – shut the door!"

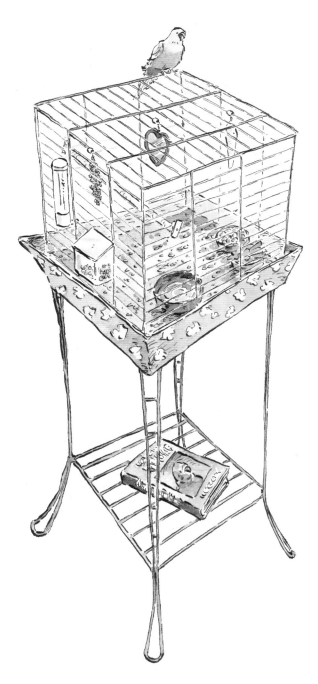

c. 700 B.C.   *c.* 640 B.C.   *c.* 500 B.C.

CHINA: lion dogs, later known as Pekingese, are popular with royalty

IRAQ: Assyrians in Nineveh train mastiff-type dogs to hunt wild pigs, lions, and antelopes

ITALY: Romans hunt rabbits with domesticated ferrets

Fin-tastic Fish

A blue-silver flash swims past, turns gracefully, and sparkles red and violet. Does it catch your imagination as well as your eye?

Beautiful colors and graceful movement may be what first hooks your interest in that fish. But the fascination deepens when you take it home. Your fish depends on you for its total life-support system – food, water, air, and shelter all in a suitable arrangement. Fresh water must always be at the correct temperature. Clean gravel, weeds, and rocks for shelter are critical, as well as the right amount of light for the proper length of time each day. With a little research, you can find tank-mates that coexist without eating each other, snails expert in aquarium cleanup, and, of course, the right kinds and amounts of food to give your particular fish. You can even discover clever ways to discourage poaching cats.

The ancient Romans were fascinated by fish, especially mustachioed sea barbels, but could house them only temporarily because they

c. 480 B.C.

GREECE: during the Persian Wars, Xanthippus's loyal dog swims alongside its master's galley from the port of Athens to the island of Salamis, a distance of about 16 km (10 mi.)

c. 380 B.C.

GREECE: Xenophon describes a strong, bristly haired dog with the astonishing ability to point at game

didn't have the technology to control water quality and temperature. For a thousand years, medieval Chinese bred colorful variations of carp, as well as fancy goldfish, in outside ponds. On special occasions, owners brought their goldfish indoors to display in porcelain bowls. Caring for fish inside, full time, only became possible when electricity was introduced into homes, just over a hundred years ago. The glass aquarium with silicone-sealed walls, filters and aerators to freshen the water, and controlled lighting has been available to the average pet-owner for about fifty years. Even today, most goldfish live a scant six to eight years in a good commercial fishbowl compared to twenty years in an aquarium or protected freshwater pond.

Kids who invest a lot of time and thought in their pets to keep them healthy enjoy creating a miniature living world and watching the shimmer as their fish swim by.

344 B.C.   326 B.C.   *c.* 324 B.C.

GREECE: twelve-year-old Alexander, son of King Philip of Macedon, tames Bucephalus, a magnificent horse the royal trainers cannot control. Alexander notices the horse is afraid of its shadow, coaxes it to face the sun, and is able to ride it

INDIA: Alexander the Great names a captured city after his beloved dog, Peritas

INDIA: a Greek soldier finds local people who keep a bird that mimics human speech. Historians think it was a large Alexandrine parakeet

How to Love a Reptile

"**B**ring-your-pet" show-and-tell was a nightmare. Daniel sneezed at birds, wept near dogs, and itched from the hamsters. Cats gave him hives. Wasn't there a pet for an allergic kid? Daniel searched the Internet for hypoallergenic pets and zoomed in on REPTILE PETS. Up popped 278,000 hits — now he had options!

Daniel discovered that a reptile would not be a conventional pet — no walks, poop and scoop, or cuddles by the fire. Most of the time, theirs would be a hands-off relationship. He'd provide the perfect home and enjoy watching his creature's day-to-day, or night-to-night, routine.

Some reptiles transmit a bacterium called salmonella and pose a health hazard. So, after cleaning the terrarium or handling a "herp" (slang for reptile or amphibian), hand-washing is essential.

Daniel learned his herp's diet should include live or recently dead food. Lizards often prefer newborn mice, but turtles will accept frozen gold-fish. His friends made faces and

218 B.C.

c. 150 B.C.

FRANCE: Hannibal crosses the Alps to attack Rome, with thousands of soldiers, thirty-seven elephants, and hounds from his home island of Ibiza, near Spain

CHINA: blue-tongued chow chows are bred for hunting, pulling sleds, and as food

squealed "gross," but Daniel informed them that this was the food chain at work.

Daniel realized his choice of herp was also limited by law. His reptile must be domestically bred – not captured in the wild. Buying domestically bred pets protects wild reptiles and prevents renegade traders from making illegal profits.

Daniel decided on a leopard gecko. This variety grows up to 28 cm (11 in.), lives happily in a 90-liter (24-gallon) terrarium, and, depending on its size, costs from $25.00 to $75.00. Geckos eat live insects, worms, grubs, and spiders, but won't turn down a small mouse. The leopard gecko has some cool characteristics, such as the ability to wet its own eyes with its tongue. Better yet, if it's scared or attacked, the end of its tail snaps off, leaving a snack behind for the predator while the gecko escapes. Daniel hopes his first herp will keep its tail, but break the record by living more than twenty-five years.

c. 50 B.C.	46 B.C.	*c.* 0 A.D.
○ CHINA: only aristocrats and royalty own pugs, one of the first lapdogs	○ ITALY: Julius Caesar has a pet giraffe	● MIDDLE EAST: Jesus is born in a stable, surrounded by domestic animals. Three men, riding camels, bring gifts

Building a Rodent Relationship

Stephanie sits, balancing the small cardboard box on her bony knees. How could her mother expect her to shop for a pet and running shoes on the same day? She can feel the hamster's little feet pattering around inside the box as the salesperson measures *her* feet. Then she hears a chewing sound and watches mesmerized as little bits of cardboard float to the floor. Soon a nose appears, followed by whiskers. "Mom! He's escaping." Once in the car, with the hamster temporarily housed inside a thick shoebox, a name pops into Stephanie's head. "Nibbles. I'll call him Nibbles."

Stephanie chose a hamster because the librarian at school had one. She liked watching Buchanan stuff his cheek pouches with his favorite treats – green peas and homemade, sugar-free oatmeal cookies. The librarian provided his food and water, but the hamster had his own sense of order. His cage was neatly divided into his toilet area, food horde, sleeping burrow, and gym. Buchanan loved being handled and

c. A.D. I	c. A.D. 50	A.D. 79

● ROMANIA: shepherds hang short, light sticks horizontally from the necks of their sheepdogs to knee level, so when they chase away intruders, the sticks bother the dogs and they return to camp before getting lost

● ITALY: Romans add one glass wall to their marble fish tanks to enhance the viewing of one of their favorite species, sea barbels

● ITALY: a dog lies across a child to save him when the city of Pompeii is smothered in volcanic ash. Years later, among the remains, archeologists find the dog's silver collar, revealing that its name was Delta and that it had saved its master, Severinus, three times

seemed to grin when his fur was combed with a soft toothbrush. Most hamsters live about three years, but Buchanan lived seven.

Stephanie wanted a pocket pet – one she could keep in her room and care for alone. Rodents such as guinea pigs and rats have similar needs, but require more space. Hedgehogs are cute, but their cages need frequent cleaning because their urine is stinky. And, they eat live insects. Feeding a carnivore was out!

At home, Stephanie introduces Nibbles to the family dog and transfers her hamster to his waiting cage. After a quick sniff of his setup – grains, water, carrot slice, gnaw toy, exercise wheel, loads of bedding – he scurries into a thick cardboard tube and packs the ends with bedding (shavings and shredded nonbleached paper towel) – it's snooze time. By evening, he's burrowing into the family routine. Nibbles hangs out in Dad's shirt pocket while Stephanie and Dad do math homework. Pocket pet, indeed.

c. A.D. 100

c. A.D. 400

ITALY: Roman ladies keep mongooses for pets

PORTUGAL: the Visigoths invade from the east with their dogs, bred to herd cattle, sheep, horses, and camels. Descendants of the breed become Portuguese water dogs, expert at herding fish into nets

17

Saddle Up!

Boots and helmet – *check*. Jodhpurs and crop – *check*. Apple for Cotishe – *check*. If your mind switches from trot to gallop at the thought of riding, you'll know why horses and ponies are included in a book about pets.

Certainly, horses were first domesticated from the wild as work and farm animals. And, over the centuries, owners bred them to enhance qualities such as speed, endurance, strength, gait, and temperament to help with work. Breeders learned that a fast-paced stallion mated to a swift mare had a good chance of producing a fleet foal. After years of breeding, there are many kinds of horses and ponies, including long, lean thorough-breds for racing; strong, quiet quarter horses for ranching; fiery, fast Arabians for chasing; large, powerful jumpers for cross-country; and strong, patient ponies for kids learning to ride.

Today, most horses and ponies are used for sport and show rather than work. And few city kids get a chance to have one to call their own.

c. A.D. 525   *c.* A.D. 550   *c.* A.D. 600

● WALES: legendary Prince Pwyll hunts on horseback with white beagles, known for their excellent sense of smell

● SWEDEN: Swedish horse riders are the first in Europe to use stirrups

● CENTRAL AMERICA: the Mayans call uo toads the pet of the rain god, Chac. Loud toad mating calls – *uoooooooh* – can be heard for great distances and signal the beginning of the rainy season

● ARABIA: the prophet Muhammad is said to have cut the sleeve off his robe rather than disturb his sleeping cat Muezza

Those who do say they have an amazing relationship. A rider speaks to her pony with words and body language, using her hands, shoulders, knees, and feet to give commands. Because ponies, when scared, want to rear or buck and run away, a rider thinks of her own safety and is sensitive to shadows, objects, and noises that might startle her mount. A rider learns to draw on her mind and body, as she sits in the saddle and holds the reins, to express confidence to her pony.

Beyond riding, kids who have ponies enjoy all sorts of connections with their pets. They love holding their pony's head while fitting the bridle straps over its ears, along its cheeks, and around its nose. They like to brush their pony down after a long ride. They don't mind pitching hay or manure, carrying water or pails of grain: a lot of work, but their reward is a soft, rumbling whinny as a thank-you.

c. A.D. **750**

CHINA: Shih Tzu, taken as tribute from Tibet, is a favored dog during the Tang Dynasty

"Gimme a Cracker Now – *Squ*awk#*!*"

In 1959, when Dorothy Hopcott took over the Caribou Hotel in Carcross, Yukon, she inherited Polly, an African gray parrot more than a hundred years old. Dorothy loved the parrot and pieced together some of its story – including the fact that Polly was likely a he.

The parrot had climbed the Chilkoot Pass into northern Canada with stampeders seeking their fortunes in the Klondike gold rush of 1898.

c. A.D. 800

IRELAND: a monk paints a cat chasing a mouse that has stolen a communion wafer on a page of sacred text in the *Book of Kells*

CHINA: fish farmers who breed small silver carp in outdoor fish-ponds watch for rare and valued yellowish orange offspring, *aka* goldfish

FRANCE: artists weave images of shaggy sheepdogs into tapestries

Polly was already fifty-two years young at the time and a long way from his original home in tropical Africa.

In 1918, Polly lived with Captain Alexander, owner of Engineer Mine. The mine's previous owner cursed Alexander's underhanded buyout tactics and wished him an early and horrible death. Sure enough, when the captain and his wife sailed to Seattle on business, their boat, the *Princess Sophia*, hit a reef in the icy waters off Alaska and sank in mountainous waves two days later. All 353 souls on board drowned. But Polly was on shore. Captain Alexander had left his par-rot at the Caribou Hotel because he didn't intend to be "outside" for long.

The owner of the hotel at the time adopted Polly and set up his perch in the restaurant's sunny east window. She cut Polly off alcohol and taught him to sing "I Love You Truly,"

c. A.D. 900

SCANDINAVIA: the Vikingarnas dogs, later Swedish Vallhunds, accompany Vikings on their sea journeys and raids
HUNGARY: the first Magyar herdsmen work sheepdogs from Asia, ancestors of the komondor and the puli

c. A.D. 950

MIDDLE EAST: elegant, long-legged salukis are permitted as companions on antelope hunts, while other dog breeds are often considered unclean

"Onward Christian Soldiers," and "Springtime in the Rockies." The parrot's conversion to clean living didn't last long – perhaps because he narrowly escaped death in two hotel fires.

By the time Dorothy inherited the parrot, Polly's habits included swearing and biting her customers, especially local gold miners. The bird also belted back whiskey until he got so drunk that he fell off his perch. Despite his wicked ways, Dorothy knew Polly loved kids – the parrot sang sweetly whenever children sat down for homemade pie in her restaurant.

With the return of winter in 1972, Polly fell off his perch for the last time. The parrot was 126 years old. Mourners came from miles away, and Dorothy laid Polly to rest under a brass plaque just outside the Carcross Cemetery, where local celebrities such as Bishop Bompass, Skookum Jim, Tagish Charlie, and Klondike Kate are buried. News of Polly's death traveled around the world. Three people sent Dorothy their old parrots to replace Polly. Scarlet O'Hara, a scarlet macaw, was already over fifty, had survived the sinking of a battleship, and liked to guzzle whiskey. Even though Scarlet O'Hara teased her cat, scolded her poodles, and bit her waitress, Dorothy loved Scarlet O'Hara to the end of his days – or maybe her days. Now Dorothy has a new parrot, Dino, guaranteed a male.

HUNGARY: a stone carver etches a huntsman carrying a falcon, accompanied by his dog, a vizsla. A thousand and one years later, vizslas join search-and-rescue teams at Ground Zero in New York

EUROPE: medieval monks are the first to breed and domesticate rabbits

RUSSIA: the first longhaired domestic cats appear near St. Petersburg, thought to be early Siberians – forebears to Persians and Angoras

ENGLAND: bear baiting and bull baiting by trained, vicious dogs are popular spectator sports

A CAT IN THE FAMILY

I'm a Cat Person

There she is – perched on the windowsill, watching for me. I bound up the stairs, wondering how she knows it's four o'clock and school's over. First she'll greet me with a nuzzle rub to the legs; then she'll mew pathetically, telling me she's hungry and bored. Even though I'm famished and my favorite show's on, I can't resist scratching her ears and filling her bowl. Kitty comes first. I'm well trained – the perfect cat person!

A cat person wishes his feet were as nimble as a cat's.

c. A.D. 1050

A.D. 1086

UNITED STATES: the Anasazi civilization has domesticated turkeys and dogs

ENGLAND: William I records a giant survey of his newly conquered land in the *Domesday Book*. Households, as well as cows, oxen, and swine, are counted

A CAT PERSON

A cat person listens for the mew, *purrrrr*, or *grrrrr*.

A cat person keeps in mind the cat thinks she's Mom — provider of all good things *and* the boss too, right?

A cat person checks out the whole animal and gauges the cat's mood — relaxed, friendly, fierce, or grumpy?

A cat person knows that nose-to-nose contact is a ticklish situation. Those whiskers are prickly!

A cat person cleans the litter box daily for one fastidious cat.

A cat person knows that even when his cat waltzes away midvisit, the cat loves him back, most of the time. . . .

A cat person always pats from head to tail, stopping to scratch at the ears, neck, back, and base of the tail.

A cat person hears *hop to it* when Kitty meows. Opens the back door. It's raining. Walks to the front door. It's raining there too.

A.D. 1162   A.D. 1165   A.D. 1228

CHINA: the empress orders a special pond constructed for her ornamental fish and declares that only royalty may keep goldfish

FRANCE: Chrétien de Troyes's condensed version of the legends of King Arthur features "chivalry," which means "horsemanship"

ITALY: Frederick II of Hohenstaufen, author of a book on the art of falconry, brings Arabian falconers home to Rome after a crusade

25

Wild Cats

Riding his bike, Tashiro rounds the corner and startles a resting cat. It hunches in the middle of the path, not moving a muscle. Not even a whisker. Tashiro's choice is to bounce onto rough ground or run over the cat. He swerves, wondering why it doesn't move. Back home, Tashiro discovers on the Internet that a threatened cat avoids predators by remaining motionless – a moving target attracts the hunter. Cats also use this tactic when creeping up on prey. They move a few steps, then remain stalk still for a long time. Guided by the same survival instincts as their forebears, domestic cats are just a few leaps in from the wild.

A.D. 1233

ITALY: Pope Gregory IX decrees that cats are instruments of the devil and orders them all to be exterminated

c. A.D. 1270

MONGOLIA: Kublai Khan has the largest kennel of dogs ever known: five thousand mastiffs

It won't surprise you that all cats come from the same original family of meat-eating, furred, clawed mammals – the *Felidae*. Over the millennia, three groups emerged: *Panthera* – all roaring cats including lions, leopards, tigers, cougars, and jaguars; *Acinonyx* – cheetahs, whose claws don't retract; and *Felis* – ancestors of the domestic cat. Fossils show that *Felis* prowled Earth before the extinction of saber-toothed cats.

Scientists researching the origins of domestic cats agree that they originated from wild cats, but from where? Many are convinced – after studying color, size, behavior, and geography – that today's North African wild cats were the predecessors of domestic cats. These wild cats look remarkably like tabby cats – irregularly striped fur with shades of red, brown, and cream, weighing about 3.6 kg (8 lb.). Independent and ferocious hunters, they live alone unless mating or raising young. Recent evidence points to another wild cat from the Middle East as a possible forebear to the domestic cat. From the deserts of the Middle East, Eurasia, or Africa, this variety's DNA matches that of modern cats.

Either way, the cat first walked into people's homes about twelve thousand years ago and has mystified its masters ever since.

A.D. 1300   *c.* A.D. 1300

ITALY: Marco Polo reports that the Chinese have the best hunting dogs in the world

THAILAND: the first Siamese cat is recorded. Now there are over fifteen varieties

WALES: farmers train their corgis to nip the heels of neighbors' cattle and pigs to drive them away from the best pastures

Who Let the Cats In?

What four-legged creature has a long tail, soft fur, whiskers, and is responsible for cats becoming pets? If you guessed a rat, you're right!

It's not known exactly when the first cat became a pet, but people needed cats when they began storing food. Historians think that about five thousand years ago, the farmers of ancient Egypt noticed wild cats preying on the pesky rats that were gobbling their grain. It wasn't long before cats were valued – even considered sacred. In an ancient Egyptian legend, Ra, the sun god, transformed into a cat and battled evil. Commonly, cats were embalmed and buried in special tombs. Citizens were even executed for harming cats. Eventually traders transported their pet felines out of Egypt to Greece and Rome, traveling with them as far east as India, China, and Japan. At the beginning of the first millennium, Roman armies spread cats throughout Europe.

But in medieval Europe, cats were feared, and their owners were thought to be witches. Cat fur was sold and their shining eyes were considered evil. Historians think that while cat numbers fell, rat numbers increased, setting the stage for the spread of the plague.

Cats finally made a comeback in the seventeenth century, when they were once again appreciated for their rodent-hunting skills. Sailing ships took cats on board to protect their cargo and food rations from rat infestations. When cats escaped or were left ashore, they quickly became feral – wild – fending for themselves at the expense of local birds and small mammals.

A.D. 1341   A.D. 1347–48

CANARY ISLANDS: Portuguese explorers capture canaries to sell in Europe as pets

EUROPE: after cats are exterminated by papal decree, rat populations explode. Fleas on rats spread the Black Death, killing one quarter of all citizens

Today, most domestic cats are pets, not rat killers. But Nature drives them to walk on the wild side as part of their daily routine. They stalk, wait, watch, and pounce when they smell a rat.

Kitty Science: Cat Senses

The first time Katie called Gran over the Internet, Roger, her cat, went berserk – rubbing his face on the microphone, trampling the keyboard, and meowing loudly. *What a pest!* When it happened again, Katie realized Roger's finely tuned senses were reacting to a familiar voice.

HEARING

Cats' amazing hearing is beyond human range. They're hypersensitive to the high-pitched or ultrasonic sounds of prey. Each ear swivels independently, moving like a satellite dish as much as 180 degrees. And because cats remember specific sounds, such as the family car's engine, they'll be waiting at the door.

What's up? Watch the ears! Tipped forward and slightly out means the cat's relaxed; ears locating sound are straight up, but twisted in one direction; ears flat against the head means the cat's defensive, but could instantly switch to attack mode.

SMELL

Cats need superior noses from birth. Before their eyes can open, kittens sniff their way to the same nipple every feed. And cats never taste food that's too hot – their noses detect temperature.

c. A.D. 1400

THAILAND: artists draw short-haired cats – Siamese, Korat, and Burmese – in seventeen illustrated poems

SIGHT

Cats have the eyes of a predator – out front for binocular vision. They predict the distance to prey and sharpen their focus by swaying their heads. Cats also have excellent peripheral – sideways – vision. Adapted for night hunting, cats need six times less light than people, but they can't see in absolute darkness.

That's where whiskers come in handy. Cats have twenty-four whiskers divided into four rows on either side of their nose. They use their whiskers like fingertips to touch and identify objects. These remarkable feelers sense air currents too, so cats can detect movement and move safely in near-dark conditions.

Whiskers also protect the eyes – if anything touches a cat's whiskers, they blink, especially when sleuthing. And, if a cat has a mouse in its jaws, the whiskers encircle the prey and give feedback to the cat. *Is dinner still moving?*

c. A.D. 1461

A.D. 1493

c. A.D. 1500

● FRANCE: Louis XI starts the fad of hunting with pure white hounds

● SPAIN: Christopher Columbus presents Queen Isabella with two parrots from Cuba

● JAPAN: aristocrats import selectively bred goldfish from China

● PERU: the Spanish discover Inca-bred guinea pigs and ship them to Europe as pets

Cat Questions

"**C**aller from Seattle, you're on the air. What's your question for Dr. Russ, our guest veterinarian?"

– *How do you explain that our cat's pupils dilate when the light hasn't changed?*

"Like ours, cats' pupils get larger as light decreases, but they also dilate when cats are stimulated or angry."

"Next caller?"

– *Our cat jumps on my lap and kneads my tummy with his sharp claws. What's he doing?*

"This is instinctive," explains Dr. Russ. "Kittens do this to stimulate their mother's milk. Cats are marking their territory."

"And from Kamloops?"

– *When our kitten meets our dog, she arches her back, sticks her tail straight up, and fluffs her fur. Then she turns sideways and hisses. Why?*

"Your cat defends herself from bigger animals by trying to appear large and fierce."

"Next question?"

– *My cat caught a mouse and played with it. Why's she so cruel?*

"Actually, your cat's primary instinct is self-preservation. Cats investigate and 'play' with prey, wearing it out so it's easier to kill."

"Now, from Whitehorse?"

c. A.D. 1500

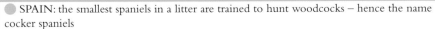

SPAIN: the smallest spaniels in a litter are trained to hunt woodcocks – hence the name cocker spaniels

ENGLAND: Dr. John Keyes suggests people cuddle up with dogs to keep warm. He thinks close contact with dogs cures stomach aches

SCOTLAND: only clan chieftains and nobles are permitted to own deerhounds, which they can use to buy their freedom if condemned to death

GERMANY: long-bodied, short-legged dachshunds are bred to help hunters dig out badgers, rabbits, and weasels from their burrows

— Why do cats scratch furniture?

"Scratching grooms the nails, is practice for catching prey, and marks a cat's territory by releasing scent from glands in the forepaws. Try offering a scratching post dusted with catnip."

"An e-mail question."

— My kitten sleeps a lot. Is this normal?

"It's called catnapping! Cats sleep five of their first seven years, or about seventeen hours a day."

"Next caller?"

— Why does our cat wind herself around our legs?

"She's rubbing you with glands on her face, leaving a scent that says *you're mine.* At the same time, she's picking up your scent that says *I'm yours.* Scientists call this scenting, but our noses can't detect these smells."

"Last caller, from Portland?"

— My cat hates it when I touch the bottoms of her feet. She leaps away and starts licking herself. What's going on?

"Cats' feet are sensitive. Handling their feet makes them feel restrained. She probably wants to bite you, but diverts her energy to grooming instead."

"Thanks, Dr. Russ!"

A.D. 1508

● ENGLAND: the word "pet" is first used to mean a tamed animal kept for pleasure

33

Talking Cat

"*Meow'm-ahh-ooh-own.*"

"What's that?"

"*Meow'm-ahh-ooh-own.*"

"Sounds like 'I'm all alone!'"

Stanley rolls on his back and purrs. *You understood perfectly. Now, please scratch the ears.*

If you watch and listen carefully, you can communicate with your cat, even though you're a different species. Cats seem to have a preprogramed vocabulary that expands depending on who's listening, making their own feelings and needs perfectly clear.

Cats usually meow to get attention — they want food, water, company, or a change of scene. Some people think the meow is reserved for cat/people relations. But a half-meow, or tiny mew, squeaks out of a kitten looking for its mother's milk.

If you waken a snoozing cat, he may greet you with what

c. A.D. 1550

CROATIA: dalmatians run alongside traveling caravans. They form a close bond with horses and are later used as coaching dogs, guarding horses that pull stagecoaches and fire engines

sounds like a question: "*Brrrrrr?*" He'll make the same sound when jumping up on your bed when it's time for breakfast. This sound can switch to "*brrr brrr,*" or "hurry up!" Cats aren't patient.

The happiest of cat sounds is the purr – it can be nearly silent, soft, or as loud as a freight train, but it means the same thing. If you're scratching his chin, keep scratching. If he's eating his food, do not disturb.

Highly stimulated, threatened, or angry cats make a range of increasingly scary sounds. A staccato "*ka ka ka*" rips from the cat that is watching a squirrel out the window. He's frustrated the prey is out of range. Spitting mad and not afraid to show it, he hisses and spits at the same time. "*Kaahhh!*" If another animal (cat, dog, or other) intrudes on his space, a domestic cat will let out a near-roar – "*Rrrrrrow!*"

When Stanley's family is washing the dishes, he jumps up on the couch and laments, "*Meow'm-ahh-ooh-own.*" English translation: *Leave the kitchen and come cuddle me.* As soon as they do, he purrs and snoozes contentedly. This happens every night. Stanley, as most cats do, likes routine.

A.D. 1561

A.D. 1588   c. A.D. 1590

A.D. 1598

FRANCE: Fouilloux publishes instructions for training low-slung basset hounds to accompany walking hunters

ENGLAND: legends claim the first tailless Manx cats swim to the Isle of Man from shipwrecked Spanish galleons. Scientists suggest that tailless-ness results from a mutation that occurred at this time

ENGLAND: Shake-speare refers to dogs in his plays, including this line from *The Merchant of Venice:* "But since I am a dog, beware my fangs."

ENGLAND: the first cat show takes place at St. Giles Fair

First You Take a Tabby

Of all domestic cats, tabbies are the most closely linked to their wild roots. For thousands of years, people didn't breed cats — kittens just happened. Over time, different breeds naturally evolved, all with some tabby in their genetic

makeup. Distinctive cats were found in specific regions: Russian Blues in Russia; the no-tailed Manx on the Isle of Man, and so on. After a famous cat show in 1871, the hobby called *cat fancy* was born.

What do cat fanciers fancy in a feline? They look at a cat — whole and in parts — and determine the breed, fancy or not.

FACES

Some cats have round faces, while others have triangular or wedge-shaped faces. A third category is the intermediate-shaped face: leaner than round, but fuller than wedged.

Look closely at your cat's eyes — are they round, oval, slanted, or slightly crossed? Cats' eyes range from dark to light in shades of orange, yellow, green, or blue. Some cats are odd-eyed, such as having one blue eye and one orange.

Depending on the breed, cat ears are pointed, rounded, curled back, or folded forward. And ears can be set close together in a V shape, perched on top or spaced wide apart.

A.D. 1602

JAPAN: a government order makes it unlawful to keep a cat indoors. Cats must live freely and feed on rodents that eat silkworms
MADAGASCAR: François Martin De Vitre describes a fascinating new reptile, the chameleon

A.D. 1603

SCOTLAND: when James VI of Scotland becomes James I of England, he sends terriers, thought to be early Scotties, from Edinburgh to a friend in France

A.D. 1620

GERMANY: a night watchman and his schnauzer are sculpted in a statue for the town square in Stuttgart

Noses vary from the long, regal Siamese to the squished pug of a Persian. The hairless nose "leather" (where the nostrils are) can be red, pink, brown, gray, black, blue, or lilac.

FUR

Cats' coats can be short-haired, long-haired, or almost hairless. The main colors are red (orange), white, black, or chestnut. Now add blue, lavender, and cream to the palette. Then mix up the colors in a pattern. Each hair can be a solid color, ticked (striped), shaded (gradually deepening in color), smoked (colored at the tip and white near the body), or tipped (colored at the tip and the rest white).

The majority of pet cats are tabbies, but distinct breeds evolved when people selectively bred cats with mutations, such as curled ears. Other breeds came from the crossing of two existing breeds, such as Persians with American shorthairs. Now there are over a hundred breeds, with thirty-nine pedigreed breeds recognized by the Cat Fancier's Association, the predominant pedigreed cat registering association in North America.

A.D. 1627

POLAND: the last auroch, the large long-horned wild ox from which cows were bred, dies in a park

You be the judge. Which cat gets top marks for appearance and personality?

MAINE COON

Adrian's cat, Alex, is the size of a large raccoon. With a thick undercoat of sand-colored fur, he sports handsome brown lines on his face and body, a lion's ruff around his neck, golden guard hairs down his back, and trousers of fluff above his hind feet. He adores his family and chirps for attention, but growls at most intruders. Adrian thinks he taught the cat to be tough, but Alex's attitude is bred in his Maine coon bones.

RAGDOLL

At the slightest commotion, Holly hides in a closet. But when hungry, she marches into the kitchen and twirls her empty food bowl with a paw.

Bold by nature, her brother, Milo, checks out anything new. Early each

morning, he rattles the bedroom blinds. If ignored, Milo climbs on the alarm clock, trampling the buttons until the radio booms. He doesn't understand "weekend."

When it comes to snuggles, Holly and Milo, with their silky rabbitlike coats, are as limp and lazy as rag dolls.

c. A.D. 1650

c. A.D. 1662

ENGLAND: hunters armed with nets and falcons use pointers to locate hares and greyhounds to chase them down

RUSSIA: aristocrats breed large beautiful hounds called borzois that can run down a wolf or hare, but are gentle companions to people

CANADA: great Pyrenees dogs guarding Basque fishing settlements cross with black English retrievers to create the Newfoundland retriever

TABBY

Nellie's a classic red tabby. Her white chin and whiskers seem to smile, but she swats the dog's nose with claws out. She loves cat grass, drinks from the dripping tap in the bathroom, and sleeps on radiators. When her family packs, she hides in the suitcases, but vomits at the sight of her own travel cage. Nellie

pesters all guests who are allergic, afraid, or who dislike cats. If you bother her while she's grooming, she'll look at you as if to say, *What're you looking at?*

SIAMESE

Steve brought home the runt of a blue point Siamese litter, with their bluish cream-colored coats, and Mom was not impressed. But Bojangles chatted his

way into the family with loud meowing conversations. And he made a cozy bed-warmer, burrowing and purring under the covers. After three months, Bojangles went missing. The Humane Society recovered a blue point that was so skinny and ratty, Steve didn't recognize him. But Lance, the family's spaniel, knew him with one sniff. From then on, Bojangles was a spoiled, indoor cat.

c. A.D. 1685

A.D. 1697

AFRICA: settlers cross their European dogs with climate-adapted local hunting dogs. Over one hundred years later, the Rhodesian ridgeback emerges, a breed capable of distracting lions while their masters hunt

EUROPE: Charles Perrault includes the fairy tale *Puss in Boots* in his *Mother Goose Tales*, helping renew cats' popularity

Pick Your Cat

A wise person once said, "Take along your money when looking for a pet cat." When you see the cute fuzzball and hear its pleading meow, you'll want to take it home. But remember, cats live about fifteen years – some live over thirty – and the cheapest thing is buying it. Food, litter, carrier, toys, catnip, and veterinary care all add up over time.

Once your family is set on having a pet feline, avoid impulse decisions by making a few choices beforehand: will it be female or male; kitten or full-grown cat; shelter or rescue center; breeder or pet store? Will it be an indoor or outdoor cat? If you live near traffic, consider indoor: chances are your cat will live twice as long. If you decide on outdoor, use a belled collar and keep it indoors from dusk to dawn, when predators (including your cat) are most active.

Before bringing your pet home, place the litter box in an accessible spot that allows both privacy for the cat and easy cleaning for you. Set up a food station, with appropriate kibble and water, in easy reach. If you have a dog, this can be tricky.

A rescued animal can make a wonderful pet, but could arrive with problems from his previous home. Ask questions! Was he abandoned, sick, or neglected when he arrived at the shelter? How old is he? Is he neutered? Spend time watching and playing with him. A friendly, outgoing personality will be a better fit with a family than a shy, skittish cat. You will be interviewed too: are there other pets in your home, very young children, enough space? Do you travel or play on a zillion sports teams? Have you the time to take good care of a cat?

c. A.D. 1700

c. A.D. 1701

● CARIBBEAN SEA: it's not known for sure if pirates such as Blackbeard owned pet parrots, but some think pirates transported exotic birds back to Europe for the menageries of the aristocracy

● CANADA: Tahltan peoples of northern British Columbia hunt bears and large cats with feisty small dogs called Tahltan bear dogs, which are now extinct

● JAPAN: a German traveler describes the Japanese bobtail cat as one that won't hunt for mice and likes to be carried

● IRELAND: Jonathan Swift finishes writing *Gulliver's Travels.* In his last voyage, Gulliver visits the land of the Houyhnhnms (elegant and refined horses that live in houses), who rule the Yahoos (stinking, vulgar humans who live in holes in the ground)

● UNITED STATES: Johannes Plott breeds a German hunting dog, known as the Plott hound, to track black bears in the wilds of North Carolina

c. A.D. 1750

c. A.D. 1770

A.D. 1777

RUSSIA, SCOTLAND, UNITED STATES: horsehair fabric – woven from horses' tails and manes – gains in popularity. Durable cloth is used in upholstery, clothing, and accessories

UNITED STATES: Maine coons are one of the first American breeds of cat. Large and strong, they have thick fur, especially on their tails

UNITED STATES: George Washington, owner of a hound named Captain, returns the dog of Britain's General Howe after the Battle of Germantown

A kitten is suckled by his mother and taught life skills for the first eight to twelve weeks of life. After that, he can leave his mother and turn your family into his family. Now, it's up to you to make a safe, healthy, and caring home for your kitten. There are no "rules" for successful cat ownership, but these common-sense guidelines will help him settle in:

- Let sleeping kittens lie. Kittens snooze a lot – your cat will choose several spots he prefers, likely where it's cozy, warm, and peaceful.
- Give your kitten space to explore on his own. Cats are naturally independent and curious. Make sure you kitty-proof, just as you would for a toddler.
- Train your kitten to keep away from "forbidden territory," such as the kitchen countertop. Use a small spray bottle filled with room-temperature water. A few squirts should be enough. Soon the sight of the spray bottle will discourage your kitty.
- Avoid car travel at first. Cats are often homebodies and can suffer from motion sickness.
- Introduce your kitten to your friends and neighbors over time. Cats hate confusion or sudden loud noises.
- Offer a buffet of fresh food and water – cats are grazers – washing the dishes with soap and water before refilling.
- Plan on lots of game time – kittens and many cats love to play. You don't need fancy toys – try making your own with bits of string or wool, balled-up foil, feathers, or Ping-Pong balls. Supervise play with homemade toys – some cats will eat them! And watch your fingers – kitty claws are sharp as razors.

c. A.D. 1780

c. A.D. 1800

FRANCE: Marie Antoinette and her courtiers pamper their pet poodles

UNITED STATES: greyhounds help hunters run down wild game on the western frontier

Mabel: A Community Cat

Every time Brett opened the door at Mabel's Fables, the hunt was on. *Where was Mabel?* His sister went straight for the new books, but he wanted to find the cat – she was the pet he couldn't have at home. Brett searched the window display, where Mabel might be monitoring the sparrows outside. She could be snoozing in a carton of books, or wide-awake at the bottom of the stairs. When he found her, he'd get the nod from Eleanor – her owner – before scratching Mabel's soft ears. Then he'd find a hockey book.

From the beginning, Eleanor and her sister knew their bookstore needed a cat. The right cat would welcome customers and move book shopping into a no-pressure comfort zone. They needed an unflappable "public" cat – calm, unfazed by sudden or scary noises, and quick to vanish when necessary. Did such a cat exist?

Mabel, mature and street-wise, filled the bill and became the furry face of the store.

People read the sign and closed the door behind them, keeping Mabel safely inside. When she escaped once, the community joined the search. Everyone was relieved when Mabel scooted in one morning and resumed her job.

A.D. 1804

A.D. 1807

A.D. 1812

UNITED STATES: William Clark, Meriwether Lewis, and Lewis's Newfoundland dog Seaman start up the Missouri River on their two-year journey of discovery into Oregon country

UNITED STATES: two puppies, rescued from a sinking ship off Maryland, are bred with local dogs to create the first Chesapeake Bay retrievers

SWITZERLAND: Barry, a search-and-rescue forebear of the modern Saint Bernard, dies. Over his working life, Barry is credited with saving forty travelers buried in the snow of the Saint Bernard Pass in the Alps

Years later, walking to high school, Brett read a notice on the door:

MABEL 1985–2002
Not a stuffed feline, but quite real
And certainly
Not a windup toy.
Mostly gentle, mostly cheerful
Always inquisitive
And the soul of our little bookstore.
Thank you, Mabel.

Brett's stomach went *clunk* and his eyes filled with tears. But like many good stories, this one has a sequel.

Eleanor scanned the caged cats at the animal shelter. *Pick me! No, me!* their bodies yowled. One bold male poked his paw through the wire, swiping at air. He wouldn't do — feisty was not in the job description. Then Eleanor stopped at the last cage. Staring back was a full-grown orange tabby. Her wise green eyes held Eleanor's, as if to say, *I pick you.* Eleanor knew she'd found Mabel Two.

c. A.D. 1820

A.D. 1822

FRANCE: Poet Gérard de Nerval walks his pet lobster in the park in Paris

CANADA: Newfoundland fishermen's dogs, with their coats of black, thick, short, water-repelling hair, are first called St. John's water dogs, later Labrador retrievers

Jasper: A Feline Survival Story

Jasper flattens his ears and twitches his tail. The empty food and water dishes, plus loads of stuff on the dock, tell the ugly truth – summer is over. After two glorious months of prowling the island, he's headed for the city.

The boat slips into the marina, and Jasper's owner revs up the engine. A resounding backfire startles everyone as Jasper screeches, jumps from the boat, and bolts. His family searches frantically and finally admits he's lost. But the

harbormaster promises to phone when the cat turns up.

Jasper runs, heart pounding, and hides in a thicket of raspberry bushes. He grooms his tail, plucking out burrs. As night falls, he circles back to the now-empty parking lot and finds his dish full of kibble. He takes a nibble and saunters to a nearby puddle for a drink. Suddenly, a sharp yip warns that a fox smells the food too. Jasper darts away as his bowl empties.

c. A.D. 1825

A.D. 1835

UNITED STATES: Carolina parakeets, North America's only native parrot, are collected as pets. Loss of habitat and collection of their eggs and feathers contribute to their extinction by 1939

ENGLAND: laws pass forbidding dog fighting, but are not enforced

For the next ten months, Jasper transforms from a pampered pet into a successful feral hunter. In September, he sticks close to the marina, meeting the school bus each day. The harbormaster's children make him a cardboard house and leave out food, but never tell their dad. Jasper catches mice, grasshoppers, and birds – anything that moves.

October brings rain and trouble. Jasper's handouts attract other wildlife, and, at twenty years old, Jasper is no match for an aggressive raccoon. As the days shorten, the children spend more time indoors and forget about the stray cat. He finally moves on.

November is long and lonely, but Jasper makes himself a home in a shed,

A.D. 1839   A.D. 1840   A.D. 1845

● SYRIA: British zoologist George Waterhouse finds a new species in the desert and calls it a golden hamster

● AUSTRALIA: John Gould captures two parakeets, later called budgies, and takes them home to England

● CANADA: Sir John Franklin and crew, on board the *Terror* and the *Erebus*, disappear forever into the Arctic, along with Franklin's dog, Neptune, and his monkey, Jacko

47

sheltered from rain and wind. Despite plentiful prey, he's losing weight. And his fur thickens and mats. One warm day, he watches a man rake leaves. Jasper follows him to his door and doesn't understand when the man says, "Sorry, buddy. I'm allergic to cats."

Finally, in December, there's something to purr about. A family with three kids and two dogs arrives at their cabin for the holidays. Despite Jasper's scruffy appearance, his collar tells them he's someone's pet. Food, a warm fire, and lots of attention are all good — but a bath?

Jasper slips back into domestic life: hunting each night, returning for breakfast and a snooze. One windy evening, snow turns to freezing rain and his yowls at the door go unheard. Soaked and cold to the bone, he hunkers down in a nearby boathouse. Even though he wraps his tail around his body, the tip suffers frostbite, snaps, and bends over. It's very painful. When Jasper returns to the cabin, the family is gone, but this time he eats the entire bowl of food they've left behind.

A.D. 1846

c. A.D. 1850

ENGLAND: Anna Thynne manages to keep corals and seaweed alive for three years in a saltwater aquarium

THAILAND: the king of Siam joins the local craze for betting on bettas, later called Siamese fighting fish

SRI LANKA: a British zoologist identifies a new species called leopard gecko

48

During the nonstop cold of January and February, prey is scarce. Along a game trail, Jasper's keen nose detects rabbit. On high alert he waits, finally sensing vibration and movement. As the bunny bounds toward him, Jasper sinks lower, preparing to pounce. *Now!* He leaps forward just as the sharp talons of a great horned owl descend from above, raking his ear before swinging the rabbit skyward. Jasper hides under a deck and licks his wounds. For good measure, he sprays strong musky urine along the perimeter of his new refuge, warning other creatures to back off.

In March, with the promise of spring, Jasper finds easy pickings under a bird-feeder, where migrants stop to refuel. A woman offers him a saucer of milk, while scolding him for eating her visitors. Jasper's not impressed when she clips a flea collar around his neck.

A.D. 1859

A.D. 1860

ENGLAND: the first formal dog show, held at Newcastle-on-Tyne, features English pointers and setters

BELGIUM: Paul Reuter, later of Reuters news agency, uses forty-five homing pigeons to send stock prices and news between Brussels, Belgium, and Aachen, Germany

A.D. 1863

A.D. 1865

A.D. 1866

SCOTLAND: teenager Alexander Graham Bell tricks people into thinking his Skye terrier, Trouve, is talking. He teaches Trouve to growl continuously while he manipulates its lips and vocal cords

SCOTLAND: Lord Tweedmouth breeds one yellow pup from a litter of black, wavy-coated retrievers with a Tweed water spaniel (now extinct) to create the first golden retrievers. His new breed tolerates the noise of shotguns and proves to be good at fetching

CANADA: three students are the first graduates from the Upper Canada Veterinary School, now known as the Ontario Veterinary College

With the good weather, locked-up buildings are opened and cleaned. Jasper explores, looking for a handout or a warm spot to rest. Close to one building, where soft earth is exposed, he finds a new food source – slow-moving insects and spiders.

An antique shop has a poster in the window, complete with photo: LOST – BELOVED FAMILY PET: BLACK FLUFFY CAT, GREEN EYES, ANSWERS TO JASPER. The man looks at the cat on his doorstep and shrugs. "Guess you're not Jasper." When Jasper meows his reply, he's rewarded with a scratch on the chin and some tuna fish.

As summer approaches, the marina bustles with life. Jasper watches from a distance, wary of all that moves. He hunts and avoids being hunted. On the first long weekend, cars roll into the lot. A rowdy pup chases Jasper up a pine tree, so he misses the arrival of his family. They talk to the harbormaster and are sad to hear Jasper never came back. Still, they leave a flyer and offer a reward for his safe return.

While they're unpacking the boat, the phone rings. It's the harbormaster, shouting that there's a cat on the dock: black, with flat, dull fur, a scar on his ear, and a bent tail. Sure enough, it's Jasper. After a wildly happy reunion with his family, he saunters to the refrigerator and meows.

Postscript: Jasper lives to be twenty-six.

A.D. 1867   A.D. 1868

UNITED STATES: the American Society for the Prevention of Cruelty to Animals launches an emergency service for injured horses

ETHIOPIA: English soldiers collect a new kind of cat, later called Abyssinian

A DOG IN THE FAMILY
I'm a Dog Person

If I say the words "walk" or "ball," my dog picks up my shoe and runs to the front door, his whole body wagging. I've started using the letters *w* and *b* instead, unless I'm ready to head straight outdoors. But he'll figure out my code soon enough – he's pretty smart. Spending time outside is what I like best, anyway. I include my dog whenever I can – I never miss Dog Day at the ballpark. I'm a dog person and he's family. For him, we're his pack. Dog people are easy to identify by their slightly crazy, dog-friendly qualities.

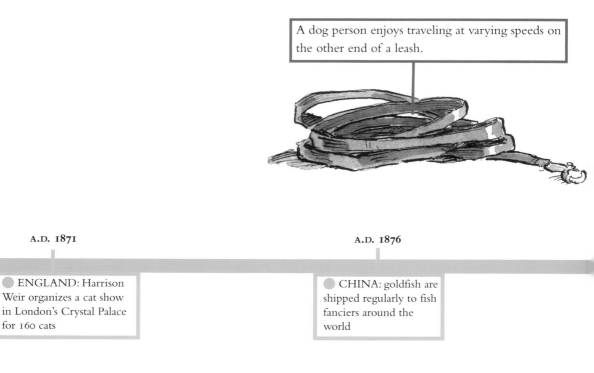

A dog person enjoys traveling at varying speeds on the other end of a leash.

A.D. 1871

● ENGLAND: Harrison Weir organizes a cat show in London's Crystal Palace for 160 cats

A.D. 1876

● CHINA: goldfish are shipped regularly to fish fanciers around the world

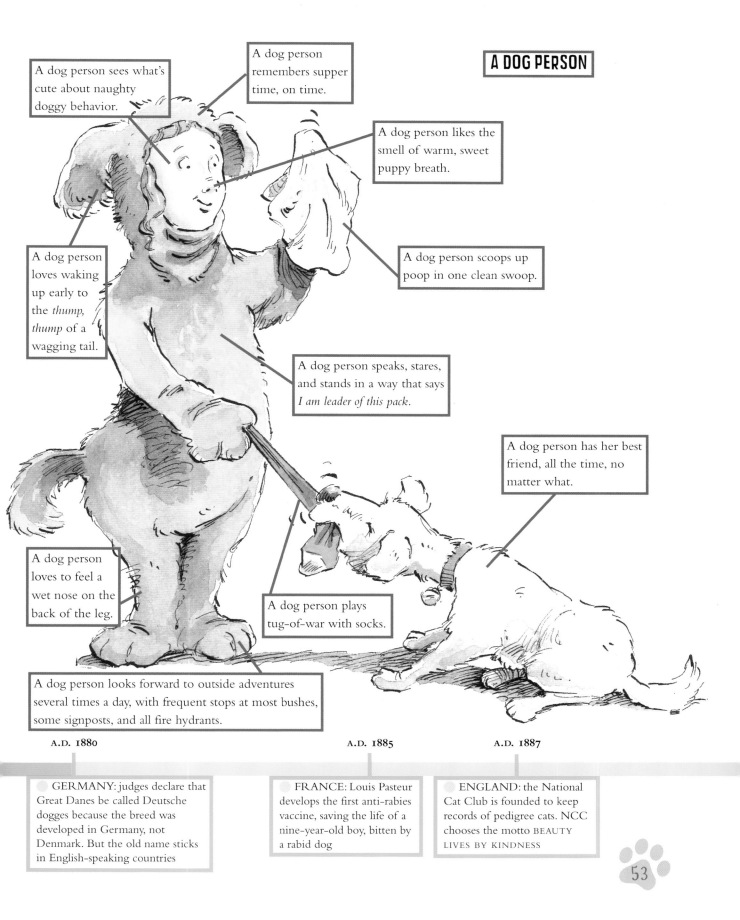

A DOG PERSON

A dog person sees what's cute about naughty doggy behavior.

A dog person remembers supper time, on time.

A dog person likes the smell of warm, sweet puppy breath.

A dog person loves waking up early to the *thump, thump* of a wagging tail.

A dog person scoops up poop in one clean swoop.

A dog person speaks, stares, and stands in a way that says *I am leader of this pack.*

A dog person has her best friend, all the time, no matter what.

A dog person loves to feel a wet nose on the back of the leg.

A dog person plays tug-of-war with socks.

A dog person looks forward to outside adventures several times a day, with frequent stops at most bushes, some signposts, and all fire hydrants.

A.D. 1880

A.D. 1885

A.D. 1887

GERMANY: judges declare that Great Danes be called Deutsche dogges because the breed was developed in Germany, not Denmark. But the old name sticks in English-speaking countries

FRANCE: Louis Pasteur develops the first anti-rabies vaccine, saving the life of a nine-year-old boy, bitten by a rabid dog

ENGLAND: the National Cat Club is founded to keep records of pedigree cats. NCC chooses the motto BEAUTY LIVES BY KINDNESS

53

Wild Dogs

Tagish barked frantically to go out on a cold winter morning. Mason opened the door and watched him jump through the deep snow into the meadow and abruptly stop. Ahead, at the edge of a stand of cedars, a fox stood frozen in its tracks, its red fur puffed and its tail pointed straight behind. Tagish looked at the fox, sniffed the air, and sat down. The fox took several steps forward, then backward, and sat down too. Mason watched the two stare at each other for several long minutes. Then the fox scratched its flank with a hind paw, stood up, and ambled back into the cedars. After it disappeared, Tagish walked over to where the fox sat, sniffed all around, rolled in the snow, and then peed. Tagish shook himself and returned to the house. As he let the dog in, Mason looked back into the meadow. The fox had slipped out of the woods and was rolling in the snow where Tagish had rolled. Then it peed and shook itself before trotting on across the meadow.

A.D. 1887

A.D. 1890

AUSTRALIA: Scottish and British terriers are crossbred to produce tough little outback snake-and-rodent-hunting Australian terriers

GERMANY: tax collector Louis Dobermann breeds muscled Doberman pinschers to protect him in his work

Foxes and domestic dogs are similar in many ways. They are members of the same mammal family, the *Canidae*, along with coyotes, jackals, African wild dogs, and wolves. All *Canidae* have large brains, bone-crushing teeth, muscular bodies, strong legs, padded feet, and walk on their toes. They have common ancestors — from the first small, doglike mammals that appeared after the dinosaurs. But of all modern-day *Canidae*, the domestic dog is most directly related to the wolf. Using DNA evidence, scientists have shown that all domestic dogs — from Chihuahuas to St. Bernards — can be traced to several packs of gray wolves that lived in East Asia, perhaps as long as one hundred thousand years ago. But archeological evidence doesn't put dogs in the human picture until about fifteen thousand years ago.

How long dogs have been separate from wolves doesn't concern Tagish — he can still tap into his wild side when he wants to.

A.D. 1893

A.D. 1894

● ENGLAND: Old Hemp is born — a border collie who wins a dog trial every year of his life, a record that has never been beaten

● UNITED STATES: Mark Twain writes, "If man could be crossed with a cat, it would improve the man but deteriorate the cat."
● AUSTRALIA: the government bans the capture and export of native birds, including parakeets and budgies

Who Let the Dogs In?

Once upon a time, a prehistoric hunter carried a wolf cub back to his family – and the story of the domestication of dogs began. At least, that is what scientists believed until recently. . . .

We now know that wolf cubs fear humans unless they are introduced by ten days of age, when they are still nursing. Would prehistoric people have had the time or know-how to successfully rear infant wolves? Scientists have found that, when only the tamest foxes are selected for breeding on fox farms, their descendants are not only less fearful of people, but they also eventually change physically – with floppier ears, curlier tails, mottled coats, smaller skulls, and shorter muzzles. Aren't these also the major physical differences between tame dogs and wild wolves? Such scientific discoveries have rewritten the old story of how dogs became domesticated. The newer version reads something like this . . .

Long ago, when prehistoric people started living in large family groups, wolves found a new food source – garbage middens near campfire circles. Being intelligent, the wolves tried to scavenge refuse; but being afraid, they snarled and snapped at any person who came close. And so, the families chased the wolves away. Then, by chance, a few wolves emerged that were less afraid of people. These wolves learned to defend the food source from intruders – other wolves, bears, even human strangers – providing much-wanted

A.D. 1895

A.D. 1896

● UNITED STATES: a Maine coon cat steals the limelight at the first cat show held at Madison Square Garden
● ENGLAND: Nipper, the dog listening to a gramophone in RCA Victor's logo, dies

● UNITED STATES: the world's first recognized pet cemetery opens in veterinarian Samuel Johnson's New York apple orchard

security for the families. The most successful of each generation of wolves were those that were the tamest with people. Being strong walkers and trackers, these tamer wolves also followed their families to new fishing and hunting camps, howling at danger along the way. Over time, their cubs or "puppies" were invited to come closer to the warm campfire and to share better cuts of meat. After many generations, the prick ears, straight tails, uniform coat colors, big heads, and long pointed noses of the tame wolves changed, and they began to look like modern dogs.

So, did people domesticate dogs, or did dogs domesticate people?

A.D. 1899

A.D. 1901

● UNITED STATES: Nick Carter, a bloodhound, is born. In his career, Nick's nose picks up trails leading to the convictions of six hundred criminals

● UNITED STATES: Teddy Roosevelt prepares to move into the White House with his family pets, including Emily Spinach the garter snake, Josiah the badger, and Algonquin the pony

Puppy Science: Dog Senses

The Dude pulls excitedly on his leash, nose to the ground, as he runs into the park – and stops. His body freezes, his legs stiffen, his ears prick, his nose twitches. Olivia follows his steady gaze and makes out, in the distance, a new dog playing with a boy in a green shirt. Does the Dude notice the same things about the newcomers as Olivia does?

Before they even get to the park, the Dude's nose picks up the newcomers – he already knows whether the dog is male or female and what it ate for breakfast. Standing in the entrance, the Dude notices the smallest maneuvers of their game, but only sees the boy's shirt as gray. While Olivia may hear the boy call out a command or two, the Dude hears sounds that the boy, right beside his dog, will never, ever hear.

A.D. 1901

ENGLAND: Sherlock Holmes tracks down a terrifying ghost dog in Sir Arthur Conan Doyle's book *The Hound of the Baskervilles*

A.D. 1903

ENGLAND: the Kennel Club recognizes the Labrador retriever as a separate breed, but declares it can never be a show champion unless certified in field trials

A.D. 1904

ENGLAND: Nana, the Newfoundland dog-nanny, is the first dog-actor to star in J.M. Barrie's play *Peter Pan*

58

SIGHT

The receptor cells at the back of dogs' eyes are more sensitive to light and movement than to color. That means dogs can detect small movements and penetrate distant and dim light better than humans. But dogs see the world in duller colors and, in fact, can't tell the difference between red and green.

HEARING

With many muscles to move their ears, dogs can locate sounds better than we can. Dogs can also hear sounds up to four times farther away and detect both lower and higher sounds than humanly possible.

SMELL

With 220 million scent receptors in their noses and on the roofs of their mouths (we have 5 million), dogs pick up smells we can't imagine. And the wetter the nose, the stronger the sense of smell. Dogs follow recent scents in the air and can pursue a ground trail many days old.

A.D. 1907

A.D. 1909

ENGLAND: Beatrix Potter publishes *The Tale of Tom Kitten*

ARCTIC: Robert E. Peary loses most of his 133 dogs on his quest to reach the North Pole

Puppy Science: Natural Born Predators

Jennifer and her dad pull on their outdoor sweaters, click into their cross-country skis, and head down the first hill with Darius, their lovable black Labrador retriever, close behind. Jennifer's dad falls at the bottom and struggles in the deep snow, with Darius licking him playfully. Then Jennifer notices a startled look cross her dad's face — he shakes his shoulders and arms violently, tears off his sweater, and throws it onto the snow. A fat, dark meadow vole runs out the sleeve. Darius jumps forward, opens his mouth, and swallows the vole whole. To Jennifer, Darius doesn't seem to bite down — he inhales the vole and carries on walking without breaking stride. Is the vole running around in Darius's gut like it did in her dad's sleeve? Poor vole!

A.D. 1911

A.D. 1912

A.D. 1914

ANTARCTICA: Roald Amundsen is the first human to reach the South Pole and return alive. He travels by dogsled pulled by Samoyeds

RUSSIA: a wealthy grand duke leads a wolf hunt that requires two freight trains to carry all his guests, servants, horses, tents, equipment, food, and over one hundred borzoi hunting dogs

EUROPE: the Red Cross uses Airedale terriers to search out wounded soldiers and carry medical supplies

Dogs are natural born predators. They have a predator's powerful body as well as killer instincts. And these both come from their forebear, the gray wolf.

Like wolves, dogs have teeth and jaws made for attacking, biting, and chewing. Their muscular forelegs have fused carpals (wrists) for extra power in chasing and fighting. Their hearts and lungs are oversized for their bodies, and their red blood cell count is high – which, altogether, make it possible for dogs to lunge into action and output high energy for a long time.

As for ancient instincts, their tendency to travel in packs gives dogs a deep loyalty and readiness to obey their human families. The wolf passed on instincts to protect the pack (family) and retrieve for it. And the predatory tactic of cutting easy prey off from the rest of a herd has transformed, in some dogs, into an amazing ability to guide, herd, and drive large numbers of livestock.

Lovable? Yes. Controlled? Yes. But don't be surprised when dogs, like Darius, will be dogs!

A.D. 1915

A.D. 1918

UNITED STATES: a cook in the South names cornmeal dumplings "hush puppies" after throwing one to a hungry, barking puppy to hush it

UNITED STATES: Scraps, a white mutt with a brown spot over one eye, stars with Charlie Chaplin in the silent movie *A Dog's Life*

Talking Dog

If you got down on your hands and knees in front of a friendly dog, raised your bottom and wiggled it, lowered your head, relaxed your mouth, looked at the dog but not right into its eyes, and breathed "*hhuhuhhuhuh*" in excited, bursting pants, your friends would probably think you'd lost it. But the dog might think you were "dog-laughing" and offering an invitation to play.

Talking dog involves making sounds as well as using body language – a powerful combo that dogs inherited from wolves. Dogs communicate status – who is leader and who is follower – as well as feelings using their body stance, voices, eyes, ears, lips, foreheads, and tails.

PLAYFULNESS

As well as a wagging tail, relaxed mouth, soft and indirect gaze, and excited pants, a dog may show its playfulness by stamping its paws back and forth, chattering its teeth, or barking in short harmonious "yarfs." It's giving a clear message: *We're going to have fun!*

---

c. A.D. 1920

SWEDEN: geneticist Dr. Tjebbes develops the Himalayan cat by breeding Persians with Siamese
GERMANY: the government trains guide dogs to help war-blinded veterans

A.D. 1921

CANADA: Dr. Frederick Banting and Charles Best keep their first diabetic patient alive with insulin – Marjorie, the mongrel dog

LEADER AND FOLLOWER

When dogs meet in the park, even as friends, the dominant one will look directly at the other dogs; hold its tail high and wag it stiffly; keep its ears lifted and forward; open its lips a little; and perhaps make a rumbly growl. More submissive dogs will avoid direct eye contact; hold their tails low, wagging in wide sweeps; lay their ears back; "smile" showing their front teeth; perhaps lick their lips and nose; and make whiny noises. The most submissive will cringe, roll over, and show their stomachs. And then all the dogs will get close and personal, sniffing each other's rear ends.

CONTENTEDNESS

A gently wagging tail, smiling mouth, half-closed eyes, and forward and flattened ears all add up to a happy and relaxed dog. A tilted head, raised ears, eager eyes, loose and fluid body, and a single bark indicate happy but ready for a little action.

Turn the page for more about talking and reading dog. . . .

A.D. 1925

A.D. 1928

UNITED STATES: sled dogs carry lifesaving serum to the remote settlement of Nome, Alaska, where people lie dying of diphtheria. One team is led by Balto, a malamute, who is commemorated with a statue in Central Park, New York

ANTARCTICA: Admiral Richard E. Byrd travels the continent with his fox terrier, Igloo

LONG-DISTANCE BLUES

Some dogs, especially working sled dogs, keep in touch by howling. Hounds on the hunt communicate with a mournful sound called baying. But a family pet in the backyard that exchanges howls with distant neighbor dogs is probably lonely.

GUILT

Although dogs may not truly feel guilt, they know when they're looking at trouble. After stealing food, eating cat litter, or shredding mail, they slink away with baleful, hangdog eyes.

ANXIETY

When a dog is unsure or a little fearful, its tail may make small, short wags and its bark will be sharp and high. It could yawn, or its head could turn to the side, but its eyes watch warily and show a lot of white.

A.D. 1931

A.D. 1932

UNITED STATES: Frank Austin patents the first pet ant farm, or formicarium

UNITED STATES: Rin Tin Tin dies. A German messenger dog, he was wounded in World War I and later starred in twenty-two movies

ANGER

An angry dog will have hard staring eyes, tail up and bristled, and raised hackles along its neck. Its head will crane forward, ears pricked, and it will not move. The dog's mouth will be open, showing front and back teeth, and it will snarl menacingly. When confronted with an angry dog, stand tall, arms and legs together, up against a wall or a tree, and don't try to run. The dog will lose interest.

Take a page from your dog's book. When you want to be obeyed, stand tall, look directly at your dog, and speak in a deep voice. When you want to send a message of "good dog," raise your voice but keep it gentle, smile and laugh a bit, and softly stroke the dog's head, sides, and chest, or rub under the ears and chin. It's important to be consistent in your actions. But when you hug your dog from the front, pat it sharply on the head, or make lots of quick movements, even in fun, you confuse it and send – not love – but aggressive, angry messages. Communicating with your dog properly is important to your relationship.

A.D. 1935

A.D. 1939

MONGOLIA: twenty pairs of gerbils are captured and bred for pets

ENGLAND: T.S. Eliot pens a collection of poems in *Old Possum's Book of Practical Cats*. *Cats*, a smash-hit musical based on the collection, opens in 1981 in London

UNITED STATES: moviegoers watch as Dorothy and her dog, Toto, are swept away in a tornado from their home in Kansas. The pair spends the whole film of *The Wizard of Oz* getting back

Nature and Nurture

Papillons, Boston terriers, Great Danes, and Newfoundlands look vastly different from one another, but are still one species – domestic dogs. Scientists think that dogs vary in size and shape because early wild dogs kept mating with wolves, adding richness to the genetic mix.

While early prehistoric dogs were uniform in size like wolves, archeologists know that by 7000 B.C., domestic dogs came in distinctly different sizes. How much of that was Nature's course and how much was early breeding by humans, we don't know. But we do know that by 3000 B.C., people understood breeding well and were probably deliberately handpicking mates for their dogs. That way they could emphasize traits they liked, such as size, color, strength, endurance, ferocity or gentleness, hair length, and the ability to do specialized work.

If you visited Rome two thousand years ago, you would recognize many generic, modern breeds – greyhounds (hunters by speed), pack hounds (hunters

A.D. 1940

UNITED STATES: three hundred collie dogs audition for the lead role in the film *Lassie Come Home*

by scent), mastiffs (fighters and guard dogs), sheepdogs (herders), and Maltese (companion dogs). About the same time in China, chow chows were pulling carts while Pekingese kept princes and princesses warm in royal households.

During the Middle Ages, Europeans developed breeds specifically for hunting birds and animals – beagles for tracking, pointers for spotting, spaniels for flushing, griffons for running down, terriers for digging out, retrievers for recovering prey from land, and poodles for retrieving from water.

In the 1800s, dog fanciers in Europe and North America started holding dog shows. Kennel clubs drew up lists of pure breeds and set standards for height, color, stance, and other attributes of each breed. Sometimes the standards were persnickety, and there was a fine line drawn between purebreds and ordinary mutts.

Today, kennel clubs around the world recognize about 170 breeds of dog, which are divided into categories that are similar to those found in Rome two thousand years ago – herding, sporting, working, hound, terrier, nonsporting, and toy. Puppy, anyone?

A.D. 1945   A.D. 1946   A.D. 1947

UNITED STATES: Jim Davis, creator of the self-centered, lazy, irritable, cartoon cat Garfield, is born. Is his first word AARRGH?

UNITED STATES: the American Cat Club recognizes six distinct breeds of cat: Abyssinian, Burmese, Manx, Persian, Siamese, and domestic shorthair

UNITED STATES: Lucenay's Peter, the dog-actor that plays Pete the Pup in most episodes of *Our Gang* (aka *The Little Rascals*), dies

UNITED STATES: lead husky Yukon King first stars in a new radio show that eventually becomes a TV series called *Sergeant Preston of the Yukon*

Purebreds and Hybrids

A great lion fell in love with a small monkey. The lion asked the gods to shrink him to the size of his beloved, without losing his lion's heart. Their offspring was the Pekingese.

– Ancient Chinese story

The Pekingese is so old a breed that its lineage is told in folktales. But we do know the pedigree of later breeds, such as the Labrador retriever. Once created, a breed is stable – all puppies look like the breed, generation after generation. If the puppies don't – horrors – they are considered mongrels. Or maybe, with careful planning, they are *hybrids*.

THE MAKING OF A PUREBRED

In the 1400s, fishermen first arrived in Newfoundland. Their dogs – hounds from France, water dogs from Portugal, and pointers from England – bred with the dogs of the aboriginal peoples. Over several hundred years, the settlers fine-tuned the crossbreeding to create the St. John's water dog. With a dense, water-repellent coat, muscled body, and oarlike tail, this dog would leap into icy waters,

A.D. 1951   A.D. 1952

SCOTLAND: Susie, a kitten born with ears that fold forward, becomes the first of the Scottish Fold breed

UNITED STATES: vice presidential candidate Richard Nixon denies he received illegal campaign funds, but admits to being given a black-and-white cocker spaniel he names Checkers

grab the float at the end of a fishnet, and swim the net ashore, hauling in the fish. In the 1800s, these dogs were taken to England, where the Earl of Malmesbury and the Duke of Buccleuch and their descendants selectively bred many litters until they created Labrador retrievers – a noble sporting purebred, even if they eat every peanut butter sandwich left at nose level!

THE MAKING OF A HYBRID

In the 1990s, American breeders started to cross Labrador retrievers with standard poodles to create a dog with a nonshedding coat for allergy sufferers. This is not a breed nor a mongrel, but a *hybrid* – labradoodles have one parent who is a Labrador retriever and one who is a poodle. Other hybrids include the peagle – Pekingese plus beagle. Yes, even the ancient and fabled Pekingese has been hybridized. And owners say it does have a lion's heart, even if it's not a purebred.

A.D. 1955

A.D. 1956

A.D. 1957

UNITED STATES: a pair of Siamese cats has minor villain roles in Walt Disney's *Lady and the Tramp*. They sing "We Are Siamese If You Please"

UNITED STATES: Dodie Smith writes *The 101 Dalmatians*, later made into Disney films in 1961 and again in 1996

RUSSIA: Laika, a mongrel from Moscow, blasts off into space in Sputnik 2. She dies of overheating and stress after only a few orbits

Puppy Love

Be advised: puppy love is for real. Look into those big liquid eyes, run your fingers down those silky ears, feel the push of that insistent little nose snuggling into your elbow, and – you're a goner. But do some research and make a plan before you go puppy shopping. Puppies grow into a ten-to-fifteen year commitment!

One of your first decisions is, *purebred, hybrid, or mongrel*? All can be wonderful pets.

- If you buy a purebred or hybrid from a breeder, it will be expensive, but you know what you're getting. You visit the kennel, see how well the dogs are cared for, and meet the mother dog.

- Pet stores sell puppies that look cute in the window, but you have to take the owner's word on lineage, kennel, and past care. Ask around and find out if the pet store has a good reputation.

- The Humane Society offers mongrels at a bargain and, very occasionally, purebreds and hybrids. Workers there will take time to interview you because they want their dogs to have a good home – this time. They can guess what mix of breeds are in the puppy and what it will look like as an adult.

A.D. 1962

A.D. 1964

UNITED STATES: Harold von Braunhut renames his novelty pet brine shrimp "sea monkeys." He markets them mostly in comic books

UNITED STATES: Caroline Kennedy, daughter of the late president, rides her pony, Macaroni, in a 4-H Club competition

POLAND: the first all-cats set of postage stamps is issued, ten familiar pet-cat poses per set

OTHER THINGS TO CONSIDER IN CHOOSING A PUPPY

- Size – Large dogs cost more to feed and need more room to move around. Big or small, most dogs require lots of outdoor exercise.
- Barking – Some breeds, including small companion dogs, yap excitedly. Husky-type dogs and hounds will howl in the backyard. If *you* don't mind, how about the neighbors?
- Shedding – Longhaired and wirehaired dogs must be groomed regularly to reduce shedding.
- Obedience – All dogs should learn basic commands, but some, such as guard dogs, need firm instruction from puppyhood to prevent serious problems.

Research carefully, make thoughtful choices, and then let yourself fall into puppy love!

A.D. 1965

A.D. 1966

● UNITED STATES: Arnold, farmer Fred Ziffel's pet pig, stars in the new TV sitcom *Green Acres*

● UNITED STATES: the first American wirehaired cat appears in a litter of short-haired cats. The wired hair looks crimped, even in the ears

Puppy Questions

"**C**aller from Cleveland, you're on the air. What's your puppy question for Trainer Sandra?"

– *How old should a puppy be before I bring him home?*

"Most puppies are ready to leave their mothers at six to eight weeks."

"Caller from Calgary?"

– *How do I teach my puppy, Portia, not to pee on the rug?*

"Set up a crate or a cage with a door that locks. The crate should be big enough to fit Portia as an adult. Inside the front of the crate, lay down an old towel and at the back, newspapers. Portia won't like to mess her den and will whine when she needs to 'go.' When she does, take her outside."

– *But that sounds cruel, crating her all the time!*

"Not all the time. Put Portia in her crate for those short periods during the day when no one is home. She's safer there. But never leave Portia alone for long in her crate – that's cruel. Someone should be in the house with a puppy most of the day and at night."

"Montreal caller?"

– *How much exercise does my Skookum need?*

"Lots, in small doses. Get Skookum on a routine around his four meals a day. When

A.D. 1972   A.D. 1973   A.D. 1975

UNITED STATES: the pit bull, a fearless fighting dog, officially takes a gentler name – American Staffordshire terrier

UNITED STATES: eighty countries sign an agreement called CITES (Convention on International Trade in Endangered Species of Wild Fauna and Flora) aimed at protecting wildlife from extinction due to the pet trade

UNITED STATES: Gary Dahl needs two weeks to write a pet rock instruction manual. He explains how to house-train a pet rock and how to make one roll over and play dead

he wakes up, he needs a stretch outside and a
pee. Next, his meal, some quiet play, a
little rest, and then a half-hour walk
before nap time in the crate. When
he wakes up, start again. . . ."

"From Cornerbrook?"

– *How do I stop Humbert from
chewing my runners?*

"Buy a strong chew toy and
give it to Humbert whenever he
chews something unsuitable. Rub
your hands around the toy often, so it
smells like you."

"Last caller, from Buffalo?"

– *When do I start obedience-training Neptune?*

"Immediately. Get Neptune used to his leash, and reward
him with praise and small treats for obeying commands such as sit, down, stay, and come."

"That's all the time we have for
Trainer Sandra."

A.D. 1981

A.D. 1984

UNITED STATES: a stray cat
with ears that curl up and back is
taken in by a family in Lakeland,
California. She produces a litter
that includes two kittens with the
same curly ears – the beginning
of the American Curl breed

CANADA: Sonny Lindner and
his dogsled team cross the finish
line in Whitehorse, Yukon, to win
the grueling twelve-day Yukon
Quest in the first reenactment of
this historic gold-rush mail run
from Fairbanks, Alaska

Dog Culture

Lolita, Melanie's elegant, white-blonde golden retriever, loved to cool off in puddles on hot days. By the end of the summer, her coat was matted and dull, with a green tinge – and she smelled funky, even after Melanie shampooed and sprayed her down repeatedly with the hose. When a friend whispered "fish dog," it was time for the groomer. Poor Lolita whimpered when Melanie walked her through the front door of the "spa," but when she re-emerged, Lolita had a

A.D. 1993

A.D. 1994

UNITED STATES: Bill Clinton becomes president and, during his time at the White House, has a cat named Socks and a chocolate Lab named Buddy

UNITED STATES: Hazel the Hedgehog appears as a comic-strip character

SWITZERLAND: Richard Scarry – creator of Dingo Dog, Sergeant Murphy, and many other animal characters in *Cars and Trucks and Things That Go* – dies

blue scarf around her neck, her coat shone, and she smelled like roses and lavender. With a grin on her face and her paws high-stepping, Lolita pranced. She looked gorgeous and she knew it. For days, every time Melanie said, "What a beautiful pup," Lolita sashayed back and forth, her head and tail high.

Sometimes dogs are just like people. We look into their eyes and see feelings we recognize. We put them on show and reward them for strutting their stuff. We cry when they suffer or die in stories and when they miraculously survive.

Most owners pamper their dogs with a few special toys and treats — but some spend amazing amounts of money on accessories, from down-filled beds and hand-painted porcelain water bowls to gem-encrusted collars. Some even send their pets to doggy summer camp. And when they die, some owners buy expensive burial plots and chiseled stone monuments.

Melanie loves it when Lolita prances with pride and shows gratitude for gifts, but she also smiles when her dog is back lolling in puddles, chilling down, and getting dog dirty.

A.D. 1997

A.D. 1998

UNITED STATES: a hairless Sphynx cat features in the Hollywood blockbuster *Austin Powers: International Man of Mystery*

TRINIDAD AND TOBAGO: Anslem Douglas releases the song "Who Let the Dogs Out," which is later sung and barked by pumped crowds at football and baseball games

Abbey and Stellar:
A Girl and Her Best Friend

Abbey watches as a joyous pack of kids her age bicycle past her home, each wearing a numbered vest and a sleek helmet. Hopefully by the next bike-a-thon, she'll have her dog. She doesn't know what breed yet — a standard poodle, a yellow Lab, or a golden retriever? But she knows she is on a waiting list, and the dog she gets will be specially trained to respond to her seizures. Abbey's doctors are hopeful that, with medication and time, her epilepsy will improve. Until then, her dog will be her ticket to ride.

While Abbey daydreams on her front step, a one-year-old yellow Labrador retriever named Stellar is in training to be a dog guide. Stellar has already spent

A.D. 1999   A.D. 2000

SINGAPORE: Dr. Zhiyaun Gong and colleagues add a gene from a fluorescent jellyfish to zebra fish and create "glofish"

GERMANY: dog-show organizers agree to disqualify rottweilers whose tails have been docked

UNITED STATES: the number of free-roaming, abandoned, and feral cats is about the same as the number of pet cats

UNITED STATES: the movie *Best in Show* pokes fun at the antics of owners at a national dog show

his first year living with a foster family, who loved him, crate-trained him, and taught him manners and basic commands. The family took Stellar everywhere they went – to the mall, to the beach, on the bus, in elevators, and along busy streets. Now he is back in the dog-guide kennels for medical checks and general observation.

Gloria, the chief seizure-dog trainer who assesses all the dogs at the facility, spots Stellar right away. He is a great dog – well socialized, stable, confident, and focused on his handler, even when there are distractions with other dogs and people. Gloria snaps up Stellar for her seizure-response program while some of his littermates are chosen for Seeing-Eye or hearing-ear training.

Stellar moves into Gloria's office for six months of intense work. Gloria uses praise and small treats to teach Stellar to bark, to fetch a portable phone,

A.D. 2005

ENGLAND: the Dog Trust counts about 105,000 stray dogs

and to push a panic button on command. Stellar walks frequently in public places with Gloria or dog-guide volunteers. He learns that when he is wearing his dog-guide uniform – coat, harness, leash – he is at work and it's no time to pee, sniff around, or approach other dogs and people.

Then Gloria pulls Abbey's file and reads the specific details of her seizures. Gloria mimics the movements and teaches Stellar to bark persistently when he sees them. Gloria also coaches Stellar to accept a full body hug for up to fifteen minutes.

When Stellar is ready, Abbey and her mother travel to the dog-guides facility for three weeks of live-in training. Stellar practices responding to Abbey's commands of "phone" and "alert," barks when Abbey acts out falling down unconscious, and lets Abbey hug him when she pretends to wake up groggily. At the same time, Abbey feeds Stellar the right amounts of food on time, brushes him, plays with him, and takes him for long walks in uniform all over town. Abbey and Stellar move in synch from the moment they meet.

When Abbey takes Stellar home, he sleeps in his crate in her bedroom, and they go everywhere together, including school. Stellar is a magnet for the other kids, but when in dog-guide uniform, he has eyes only for Abbey.

On the tenth day back, Abbey suffers a major seizure at school. Stellar responds on cue. He barks as soon as Abbey's hands shake and keeps barking, even after she falls down unconscious, until help arrives. While the teacher clears the area and offers first aid, Stellar lies beside Abbey. As Abbey slowly wakes up, he positions himself so she can hug him for support.

Everything changes for Abbey after that. She asks the bike-a-thon kids if she and her mom, on a tandem bike and with Stellar in a sidecar, can practice with them. The kids are delighted. After a few rides, Stellar decides to run beside Abbey rather than sit out the action.

Then, incredibly, Stellar starts to bark warnings when Abbey is about to have

UNITED STATES: Oscar, a two-year-old cat, patrols the halls of a Rhode Island nursing home and identifies dying patients by sitting beside them a seizure, even before her first visible symptom. Abbey's doctors can't explain how or why, but know some dogs can sense a seizure coming. They say if Stellar keeps it up, Abbey can ride solo on her own bike.

Abbey can't think of anything better than a normal life, thanks to her amazing dog.

A.D. 2008

A.D. 2009

UNITED STATES: an estimated 5 million rabbits live as pets

CANADA: the owner of a chocolate Lab offers (and pays) $15,000 for the return of his dog, stolen while he is shopping in a convenience store

CYBERSPACE: a Google Internet search produces over 779,000 hits for aquarium screensavers

CANADA: Dog Guides Canada supports over sixteen hundred trained Seeing-Eye, hearing-ear, special-skills, and seizure-response dogs in homes across the country